More Cajun Cooking

Edited by Wendy Lazor

Modern Publishing
A Division of Unisystems, Inc.
New York, New York 10022

Printed in the U.S.A.

INTRODUCTION

Use any one of the sixteen carefully selected titles in the easy-to-read **Convenient Cooking**™ series to prepare simple or exotic meals, to learn new culinary skills or to enhance those you already have.

Learn to bake cakes in your microwave, prepare delicious meals with vegetables, or tantalizing low calorie recipes complete with calorie count for each portion. Contemplate dozens of new ideas for lunches and snacks, wake up your tastebuds with Cajun cooking, or follow any of the easy baking recipes for luscious pies and cakes. You can have a hearty meal in minutes or receive raves for making your own fresh pasta.

From appetizers to desserts, you will be delighted with the recipes in the **Convenient Cooking**™ series, the only series any cook really needs.

Welcome to the family of **Convenient Cooking**™.

BARBECUED PORK RIBS

Ingredients:

1 tablespoon margarine
1/4 cup onion, chopped
1/4 cup green pepper
1 cup catsup
1 teaspoon garlic powder
1 teaspoon black pepper
1 teaspoon ground ginger
2 tablespoons honey
1 pound pork spareribs

Directions:

Preheat oven to 350°F. Melt margarine in a medium-sized skillet. Add onion and green pepper and cook until tender. Add catsup, garlic powder, pepper, ginger and honey. Mix well. Heat thoroughly. Spray a baking sheet with no-stick cooking spray. Place ribs on baking dish. Bake for 20 minutes. Brush ribs with sauce and bake for 20 minutes more. Turn over and brush with barbecue sauce. Cook another 20 minutes. Serve warm.

Yield: 4 servings
Preparation time: 1 1/2 hours

CAJUN PITA CHIPS

Ingredients:

4 (8-inch) pita rounds
1 tablespoon margarine, melted
1 teaspoon salt
1/2 teaspoon black pepper
1/2 teaspoon cayenne pepper
1 teaspoon hot pepper flakes
1/2 teaspoon garlic powder
1/2 teaspoon dried basil

Directions:

Preheat oven to 350°F. Cut pitas in half horizontally. Cut into 4 equal portions. Separate into 32 pieces. Place on an ungreased baking sheet. Brush with melted margarine. Combine salt, black pepper, cayenne pepper, pepper flakes, garlic powder and basil in a small bowl. Sprinkle over pita chips. Bake for 10 minutes or until chips become crisp.

Yield: 32 chips
Preparation time: 30 minutes

BARBECUED CHICKEN WINGS

Ingredients:

1   tablespoon margarine
1/4 cup onion, chopped
1/4 cup green pepper
1   cup catsup
1   teaspoon garlic
    powder
1   teaspoon black pepper
1   teaspoon ground
    ginger
2   tablespoons brown
    sugar
1   pound chicken wings

Directions:

Preheat oven to 350°F. Melt margarine in a medium-sized skillet. Add onion and green pepper and cook until tender. Add catsup, garlic powder, pepper, ginger and brown sugar. Mix well. Heat thoroughly. Spray a baking sheet with no-stick cooking spray. Place chicken wings on baking dish. Brush barbecue sauce over wings. Bake for 20 minutes. Turn over, brush with barbecue sauce and cook another 10 minutes. Serve with blue cheese dressing and celery.

Yield: 4 servings
Preparation time: 30 minutes

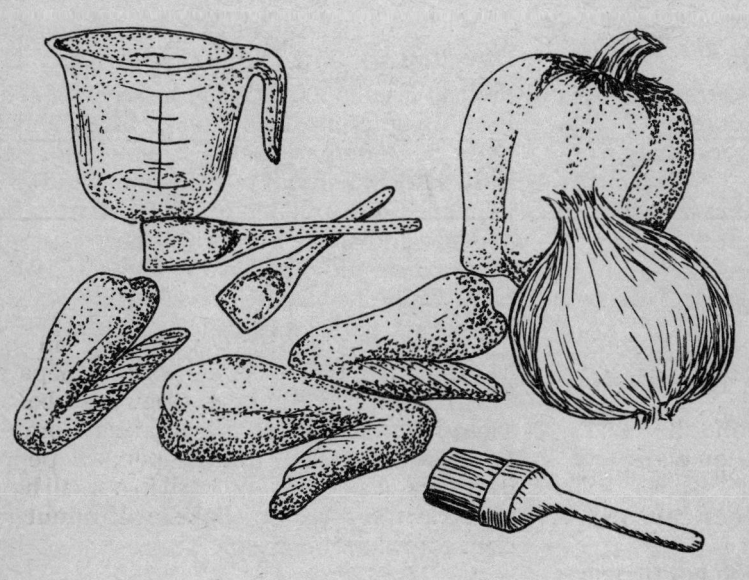

GINGER TEA

Ingredients:

4 tea bags
1 teaspoon ginger
1 teaspoon nutmeg
1 quart hot water

Directions:

Place tea bags, ginger and nutmeg in water. Let cool and reach desired strength. Serve over ice.

Yield: 4 servings
Preparation time: 1 hour

CAJUN STYLE CRABBIE MUSHROOMS

Ingredients:

12 large stuffing
   mushrooms
1 tablespoon margarine
   or oil
1/4 cup onions, chopped
1/4 cup green pepper
   chopped
1 (6 1/2-ounce) can crab
   meat
1/2 cup Parmesan
   cheese, freshly grated
1 teaspoon hot pepper
   flakes
1 teaspoon sweet basil
1/2 teaspoon black
   pepper
1 teaspoon garlic
   powder

Directions:

Preheat oven to 350°F. Wash and remove stems from mushrooms. Chop stems finely and set aside. Heat margarine or oil in a medium-sized skillet. Add mushroom stems, onions and green peppers. Cook until tender. Remove from heat and add crab meat. Stuff mushroom caps with this mixture and place on an ungreased baking dish. Combine cheese, pepper flakes, basil, pepper and garlic in a small bowl. Sprinkle over mushrooms. Bake for 20 minutes or until thoroughly cooked.

Yield: 12 mushrooms
Preparation time: 35 minutes

HOT AND SPICY CHICKEN WINGS

Ingredients:

1 (8-ounce) can tomato sauce
2 teaspoons red pepper flakes
2 teaspoons hot sauce
1 teaspoon garlic powder
1 teaspoon onion powder
2 tablespoons Jalapeño peppers, chopped
1 pound chicken wings

Directions:

Combine tomato sauce, red pepper flakes, hot sauce, garlic powder, onion powder and Jalapeño peppers in a medium-sized bowl. Mix well. Spray a baking sheet with no-stick cooking spray. Place chicken wings on baking dish. Brush barbecue sauce over wings. Bake for 20 minutes. Turn over and brush with barbecue sauce and cook another 10 minutes. Serve with blue cheese dressing and celery if desired.

Yield: 4 servings
Preparation time: 30 minutes

HOT AND SPICY RIBS

Ingredients:

1 (8-ounce) can tomato sauce
2 teaspoons cayenne pepper
2 teaspoons hot sauce
1 teaspoon garlic powder
1 teaspoon onion powder
2 tablespoons Jalapeño peppers, chopped
1 pound pork spareribs

Directions:

Combine tomato sauce, cayenne pepper, hot sauce, garlic powder, onion powder and Jalapeño peppers in a medium-sized bowl. Mix well. Spray a baking sheet with no-stick cooking spray. Place ribs on baking dish. Bake for 20 minutes. Brush ribs with sauce and bake for 20 minutes. Turn over and brush with barbecue sauce and cook another 20 minutes. Serve warm.

Yield: 4 servings
Preparation time: 30 minutes

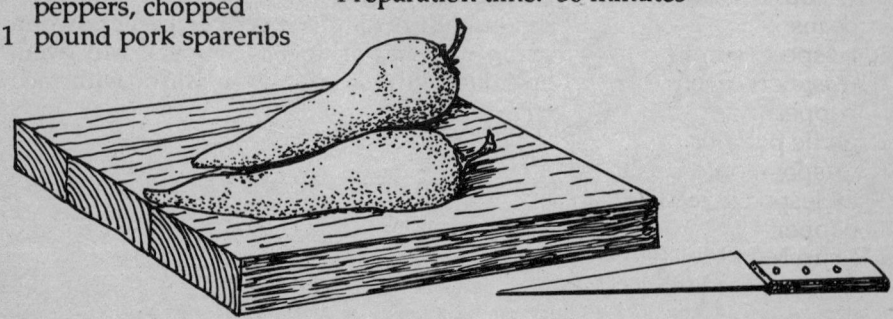

SHRIMP STUFFED MUSHROOMS

Ingredients:

12 large stuffing
  mushrooms
1 tablespoon margarine
  or oil
1/4 cup onion, chopped
1/4 cup sweet red
  pepper, chopped
1 (6 1/2-ounce) can
  shrimp
1/2 cup Romano cheese,
  freshly grated
1 teaspoon cumin
1 teaspoon dried parsley
1/2 teaspoon white
  pepper
1 teaspoon dried
  oregano leaves

Directions:

Preheat oven to 350°F. Wash and remove stems
from mushrooms. Chop stems finely and set
aside. Heat margarine or oil in a medium-sized
skillet. Add mushroom stems, onions and red
peppers. Cook until tender. Remove from heat
and add shrimp. Stuff mushroom caps with
this mixture and place on an ungreased baking
dish. Combine cheese, cumin, parsley, pepper
and oregano in a small bowl. Sprinkle over
mushrooms. Bake for 20 minutes or until
thoroughly cooked.

Yield: 12 mushrooms
Preparation time: 35 minutes

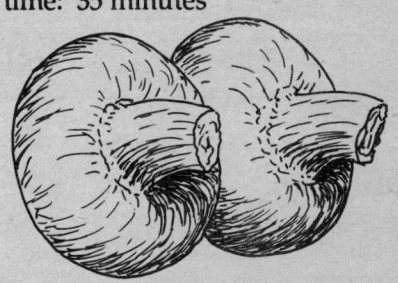

SPICY BEAN DIP

Ingredients:

1 (16-ounce) can refried
  beans
1 teaspoon cumin
1 teaspoon cayenne
  pepper
1 garlic powder
1 teaspoon onion, salt
2 tablespoons Jalapeño
  peppers
1/2 cup Monterey Jack
  cheese, shredded

Directions:

Place beans in a medium-sized saucepan. Heat
thoroughly. Add cumin, pepper, garlic powder,
onion salt and Jalapeño peppers. Mix well.
Sprinkle with cheese. Serve warm with taco
chips.

Yield: 2 cups
Preparation time: 20 minutes

SPICY HOT SHRIMP COCKTAIL

Ingredients:

1   cup catsup
1 1/2 tablespoons
    horseradish
2   tablespoons lemon
    juice
2   teaspoons chili
    powder
1   teaspoon hot sauce
1   teaspoon garlic
    powder
1/2 teaspoon cayenne
    pepper
1   pound fresh shrimp,
    cooked, drained and
    cooled

Directions:

Combine catsup, horseradish, lemon juice, chili powder, hot sauce, garlic powder and cayenne pepper in a medium-sized bowl. Mix well. Cover and refrigerate for 1 hour. Serve with shrimp.

Yield: 1 1/2 cups
Preparation time: 15 minutes

SPICY MUSTARD DIP

Ingredients:

1   pint sour cream
2   tablespoons Dijon
    style mustard
1   teaspoon salt
1   teaspoon cayenne
    pepper
1   teaspoon onion
    powder
3/4 teaspoon hot sauce
1   teaspoon dried parsley

Directions:

Combine sour cream, mustard, salt, pepper, cayenne pepper, onion powder, hot sauce and parsley in a medium-sized mixing bowl. Mix well. Cover and refrigerate for 2 hours. Serve with vegetable crudité.

Yield: 2 cups
Preparation time: 2 1/2 hours

TACO CHIPS

Ingredients:

6 corn tortillas
1 teaspoon salt
1 teaspoon chili powder
1 teaspoon cumin
1 teaspoon garlic powder

Directions:

Preheat oven to 350°F. Cut tortilla into 4 equal portions. Place on an ungreased baking sheet. Combine salt, chili powder, cumin and garlic powder in a small bowl. Sprinkle over tortillas. Bake for 10 minutes or until chips are crisp.

Yield: 24 chips
Preparation time: 20 minutes

SPICY NACHOS

Ingredients:

24 Taco chips (page 11)
1 (16-ounce) can refried beans
1 cup Monterey Jack cheese
2 tablespoons Jalapeño peppers, chopped
2 tablespoons scallions

Directions:

Preheat oven to 350°F. Place taco chips on an ungreased baking sheet. Spread a layer of refried beans over each chip. Sprinkle with cheese, peppers and scallions. Bake for 10 minutes or until cheese is melted.

Yield: 24 nachos
Preparation time: 30 minutes

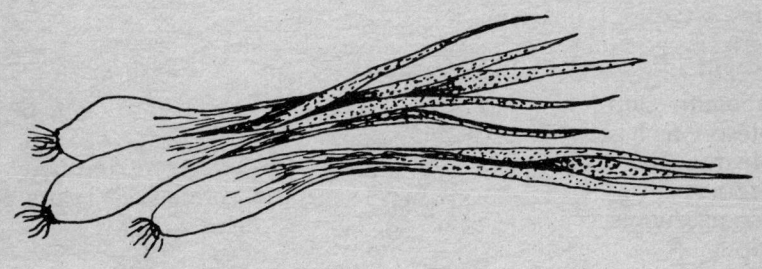

BUTTERMILK DRESSING

Ingredients:
3/4 cup buttermilk
1/2 cup mayonnaise
1 teaspoon garlic powder
1 teaspoon onion powder
1 teaspoon dried parsley
1 tablespoon chopped chives

Directions:
Combine buttermilk, mayonnaise, garlic powder, onion powder, parsley and chives in a medium-sized mixing bowl. Mix well. Cover and refrigerate until ready to use. Serve as a dressing for your favorite salad.

Yield: 1 1/2 cups
Preparation time: 30 minutes

CAJUN CHICKEN SALAD

Ingredients:
2 cups cooked chicken, chunked
1 tablespoon lemon juice
1 teaspoon cayenne pepper
1 teaspoon garlic powder
1/2 teaspoon white pepper
1 teaspoon dried basil
1/4 teaspoon dried thyme leaves
2 cups iceberg lettuce, torn into 1-inch pieces
1 cup romaine lettuce, cut into 1-inch pieces
1 medium green pepper, chopped
1 cup mushrooms, sliced
1 cup cauliflower flowerets
1 cup grated carrots
1/2 cup sunflower seeds

Directions:
Combine chicken, lemon juice, cayenne pepper, garlic powder, white pepper, basil and thyme in a medium-sized mixing bowl. Mix well. Cover and refrigerate for 1 hour. Combine lettuces, green pepper, cauliflower, mushrooms, carrots and scallions in a large salad bowl. Toss to distribute evenly. Add chicken (including marinade). Sprinkle with sunflower seeds.

Yield: 6 servings
Preparation time: 1 1/2 hours

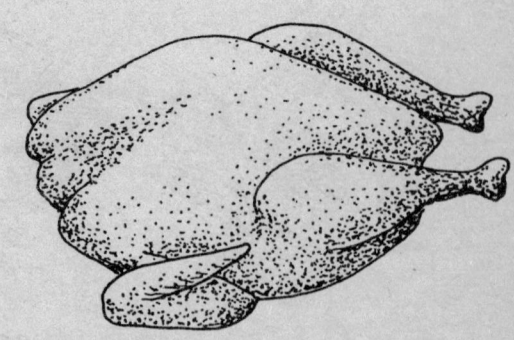

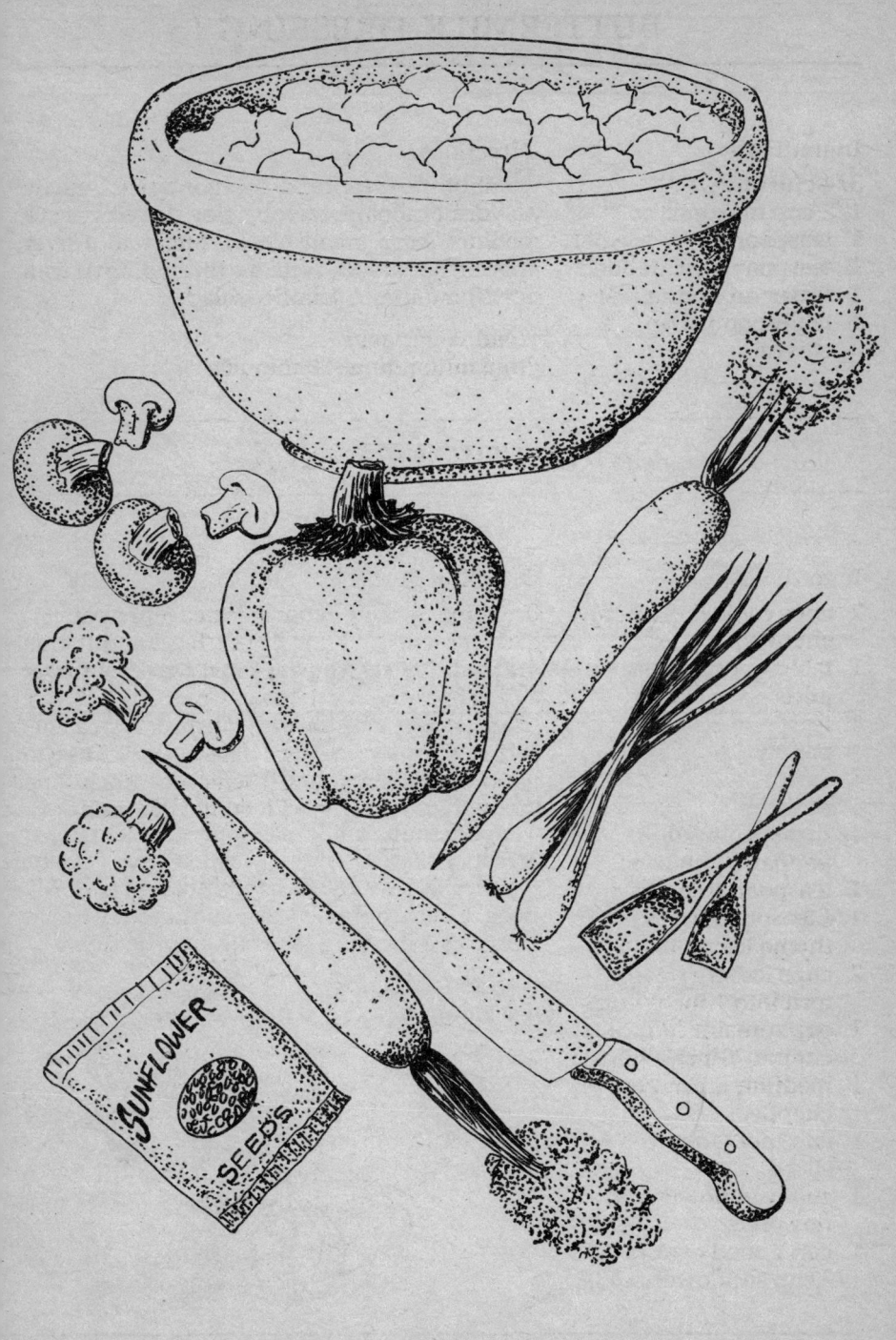

CAJUN STYLE COLESLAW

Ingredients:

4 cups cabbage,
 shredded
1 cup carrots, shredded
3/4 cup salad dressing
1 teaspoon garlic
 powder
1 teaspoon dried chives
1/2 teaspoon black
 pepper
1 teaspoon paprika

Directions:

Combine cabbage, carrots, salad dressing, garlic powder, chives and black pepper in a large mixing bowl. Mix well. Cover and refrigerate for 30 minutes. Sprinkle with paprika.

Yield: 6 servings
Preparation time: 1 hour

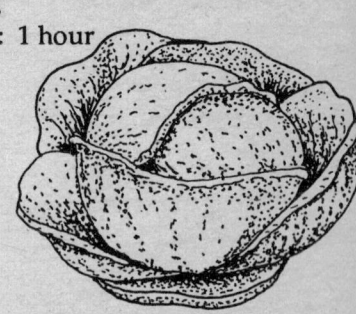

CREAMY PEPPERCORN DRESSING

Ingredients:

3/4 cup buttermilk
1/2 cup mayonnaise
2 teaspoons freshly
 ground black pepper
1 teaspoon garlic
 powder
1 teaspoon onion
 powder
1/2 teaspoon cayenne
 pepper

Directions:

Combine buttermilk, mayonnaise, black pepper, garlic powder, onion powder and cayenne pepper in a medium-sized mixing bowl. Mix well. Cover and refrigerate until ready to use. Serve as a dressing for your favorite salad.

Yield: 1 1/2 cups
Preparation time: 30 minutes

GREEN SALAD

Ingredients:

3 cups iceberg lettuce, torn into 1-inch pieces
1 medium tomato, chopped
1 cup broccoli flowerets
1 cup mushrooms, sliced
1 cup carrots, grated
1/4 cup scallions
1/2 cup chopped walnuts
1 cup Spicy Vinaigrette Dressing (page 20)

Directions:

Combine lettuce, tomato, broccoli, mushrooms, carrots, scallions and walnuts in a large salad bowl. Toss to distribute evenly. Pour Spicy Vinaigrette Dressing over.

Yield: 6 servings
Preparation time: 30 minutes

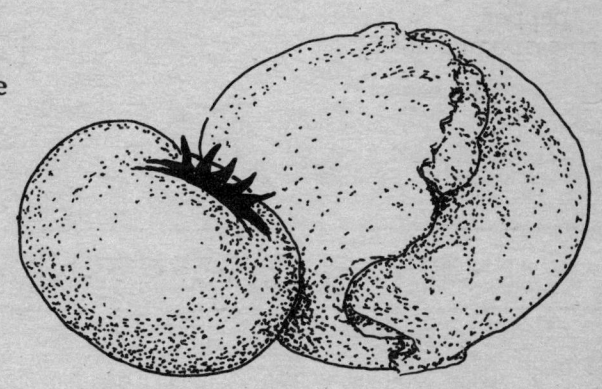

HOT PEPPER DRESSING

Ingredients:

1/4 cup red wine vinegar
2 tablespoons olive oil
1 teaspoon hot pepper flakes
1 teaspoon hot sauce
1 teaspoon garlic powder
1/2 teaspoon black pepper

Directions:

Combine vinegar, oil, red pepper flakes, hot sauce, garlic powder and black pepper in a small bowl or cruet. Mix well. Use as a dressing for your favorite salad.

Yield: 1 cup
Preparation time: 10 minutes

MARINATED BEAN SALAD

Ingredients:

1   (16-ounce) can kidney
    beans, drained
1   (16-ounce) can black
    beans, drained
1/4 cup green onion,
    chopped
1/4 cup red wine vinegar
1   teaspoon hot pepper
    flakes
1   teaspoon white
    pepper
1   teaspoon ground
    cumin
1/2 teaspoon salt
1   teaspoon dried parsley

Directions:

Combine kidney beans, black beans, onion, vinegar, pepper flakes, pepper, cumin and salt in a medium-sized mixing bowl. Toss lightly to mix well. Cover and refrigerate for 2 hours. Sprinkle with parsley before serving.

Yield: 6 servings
Preparation time: 2 1/2 hours

MARINATED CUCUMBER SALAD

Ingredients:

2 medium cucumbers, sliced
1/4 cup onion, chopped
1/4 cup vinegar
1 teaspoon cayenne pepper
1 teaspoon garlic powder
1/2 teaspoon black pepper
1/2 teaspoon dried basil leaves
6 lettuce leaves

Directions:

Place cucumbers in a large shallow dish. Combine onions, vinegar, cayenne pepper, garlic powder, black pepper and dried basil in a small bowl. Mix well. Pour over cucumbers. Cover and refrigerate for 30 minutes. Serve over lettuce leaves.

Yield: 6 servings
Preparation time: 1 hour

POTATO SALAD

Ingredients:

4 medium potatoes, peeled and chopped
1/2 cup celery, chopped
1/2 cup carrots, chopped
1/4 cup white wine vinegar
1 teaspoon black pepper
1 teaspoon garlic powder
1 teaspoon dried parsley
1/2 teaspoon red pepper flakes
1 teaspoon dry mustard
1 cup mayonnaise
2 hard boiled eggs, chopped

Directions:

Cook potatoes in boiling water for 20 minutes or until tender. Do not overcook. Drain and let cool. Place in a large bowl. Add celery, carrots, pepper, garlic powder, dried parsley, red pepper flakes, mustard and mayonnaise. Mix well. Gently fold in eggs. Cover and refrigerate for 1 hour.

Yield: 4 cups
Preparation time: 1 1/2 hours

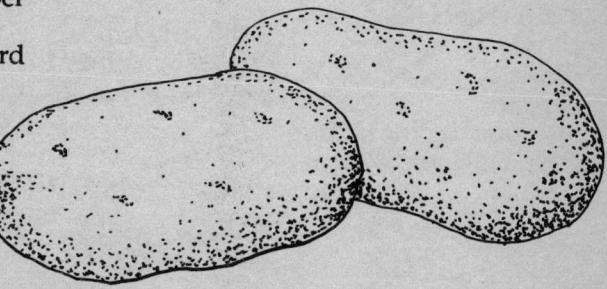

SEAFOOD SALAD

Ingredients:

1 (6 1/2-ounce) can shrimp, drained
1 (6 1/2-ounce) can crab meat, drained
3/4 cup mayonnaise
1/4 cup sour cream
1/4 cup green onion, chopped
1/4 cup sweet red pepper, chopped
1 teaspoon garlic powder
1 teaspoon dried basil
1/2 teaspoon thyme
1/4 teaspoon white pepper
4 lettuce leaves

Directions:

Combine shrimp, crab meat, mayonnaise, sour cream, green onion, sweet pepper, garlic powder, basil, thyme and white pepper in a medium-sized bowl. Mix well. Cover and refrigerate for 30 minutes. Serve on top of lettuce leaves.

Yield: 1 1/2 cups
Preparation time: 1 hour

SPICY CHICKEN SALAD

Ingredients:

2 cups cooked chicken, chunked
3/4 cup mayonnaise
1/4 cup green onion, chopped
1/4 cup water chestnuts, sliced
1/2 teaspoon cayenne pepper
1 teaspoon dry mustard
1 teaspoon garlic powder
4 lettuce leaves

Directions:

Combine chicken, mayonnaise, green onions, water chestnuts, cayenne pepper, dry mustard and garlic powder in a medium-sized bowl. Mix well. Cover and refrigerate for 30 minutes. Serve on top of lettuce leaves.

Yield: 1 1/2 cups
Preparation time: 1 hour

SPICY HOT TURKEY SALAD

Ingredients:

3 cups Green Salad (page 15)
2 cups cooked turkey, chunked
1 cup Hot Pepper Dressing (page 15)

Directions:

Place Green Salad in a large bowl. Add turkey, and mix well. Pour dressing over salad. Toss lightly to distribute.

Yield: 3 cups
Preparation time: 30 minutes

SPICY VINAIGRETTE DRESSING

Ingredients:

1/4 cup red wine vinegar
2 tablespoons olive oil
1 teaspoon garlic powder
1 teaspoon cayenne pepper
1/2 teaspoon dried basil
1 teaspoon dry mustard
1 teaspoon black pepper
1/4 teaspoon filé powder (optional)

Directions:

Combine vinegar, oil, cayenne pepper, basil, mustard, black pepper and filé powder in a small bowl or cruet. Mix well. Use as a dressing for your favorite salad.

Yield: 1 cup
Preparation time: 10 minutes

TUNA SALAD

Ingredients:
2   (6 1/2-ounce) cans
     tuna, drained
3/4 cup mayonnaise
1   teaspoon dry mustard
1   cup celery, chopped
1   teaspoon onion
     powder
1/2 teaspoon cayenne
     pepper
1   teaspoon garlic
4   lettuce leaves

Directions:
Combine tuna, mayonnaise, mustard, celery, onion powder, cayenne pepper and garlic in a medium-sized mixing bowl. Mix well. Cover and refrigerate for 30 minutes. Serve on top of lettuce leaves.

Yield: 2 cups
Preparation time: 1 hour

TUNA SALAD VINAIGRETTE

Ingredients:
3   cups Green Salad
     (page 15)
2   (6 1/2-ounce) cans
     tuna, drained
1   cup vinaigrette
     dressing (page 20)

Directions:
Place Green Salad in a large bowl. Add tuna, and mix well. Pour dressing over salad. Toss lightly to distribute.

Yield: 3 cups
Preparation time: 30 minutes

BEEF AND RICE SOUP

Ingredients:

4 cups beef broth
2 cups cooked cubed beef
1 cup carrots, chopped
1/2 cup green pepper, chopped
2 cups cooked rice
1 teaspoon red pepper flakes
1 teaspoon white pepper
1/2 teaspoon ground cumin
1 teaspoon garlic powder
1 teaspoon onion powder
1/2 teaspoon dried basil

Directions:

Combine beef broth, beef, carrots and green pepper in a large saucepan. Heat until boiling. Reduce heat, cover and simmer for 10 minutes. Add rice, pepper flakes, white pepper, cumin, garlic powder, onion powder and basil. Cover and simmer for 30 minutes.

Yield: 6 servings
Preparation time: 1 hour

BEEF GUMBO

Ingredients:

1   pound round steak,
    cut into 1-inch pieces
1/2 teaspoon cayenne
    pepper
1/4 cup vegetable oil
1/4 cup all-purpose flour
1/4 cup onion, chopped
1/4 cup sweet red
    pepper, chopped
1   cup carrots, chopped
1   teaspoon garlic powder
2   quarts hot water
1   cup beef broth
2   tablespoons filé
    powder, (optional)
2   cups cooked rice

Directions:

Sprinkle beef with cayenne pepper. Heat oil in a large saucepan. Add round steak and brown. Remove beef. Add flour to oil and stir constantly until mixture becomes darker, about 5 minutes. Remove from heat. Add onion, red pepper, carrots and garlic powder. Mix well. Return to heat and let simmer for 10 minutes. Gradually add water, beef broth and round steak and bring to a boil. Reduce heat and cover. Simmer for 1 hour. Remove from heat and stir in filé. Serve over cooked rice.

Yield: 6 servings
Preparation time: 2 hours

BLACK BEAN CHILI

Ingredients:

1   (16-ounce) can black
    beans
2   cups cooked ham,
    cubed
2   cups chicken broth
1   cup water
1/4 cup onion, chopped
1/4 cup celery, chopped
1/4 cup sweet red
    pepper, chopped
1   teaspoon garlic powder
1/2 teaspoon sweet basil
1   teaspoon cayenne
    pepper
1/2 teaspoon black pepper
1   tablespoon lemon juice

Directions:

Combine black beans, bean liquid, ham, chicken broth, water, onion, celery and sweet pepper in a medium-sized saucepan. Heat until boiling. Reduce heat, cover and simmer for 10 minutes. Add garlic powder, basil, cayenne powder, black pepper and lemon juice. Cover and simmer for 30 minutes.

Yield: 6 servings
Preparation time: 1 hour

CAJUN BEEF STEW

Ingredients:

1   teaspoon cayenne
    pepper
1   pound beef stew meat,
    cut into 1-inch cubes
1   1/2 tablespoons
    vegetable oil
1/2 cup onion, chopped
1   clove garlic, minced
3   cups beef broth
1/4 teaspoon white pepper
1   teaspoon dried thyme
    leaves
1   teaspoon hot sauce
3   medium potatoes,
    unpeeled and chopped
1   cup carrots, sliced
1   cup celery, chopped

Directions:

Sprinkle cayenne pepper over meat. Heat oil in a large saucepan. Add stew meat and cook until browned. Add onion, garlic and beef broth. Heat to boiling. Reduce heat and add pepper, thyme leaves, and hot sauce. Cover and simmer for 1 hour. Add potatoes, carrots and celery. Cover and cook an additional 30 minutes. Combine flour and water and add to stew. Stir until mixture thickens and becomes bubbly, about 2 minutes.

Yield: 6 servings
Preparation time: 2 hours

CAJUN CHICKEN STEW

Ingredients:

1   teaspoon red pepper
    flakes
1   pound chicken, cut
    into 1-inch pieces
1   1/2 tablespoons
    vegetable oil
1/2 cup onion, chopped
1   clove garlic, minced
3   cups chicken broth
1/4 teaspoon black pepper
1   teaspoon dried sweet
    basil leaves
1   teaspoon hot sauce
3   medium potatoes,
    unpeeled and chopped
1   cup carrots, sliced
1   cup celery, chopped
1/4 cup flour
1/2 cup water

Directions:

Sprinkle red pepper flakes over chicken. Heat oil in a large saucepan. Add chicken and cook until browned. Add onion, garlic and chicken broth. Heat to boiling. Reduce heat and add pepper, basil leaves and hot sauce. Cover and simmer for 1 hour. Add potatoes, carrots and celery. Cover and cook an additional 30 minutes. Combine flour and water and add to stew. Stir until mixture thickens and becomes bubbly, about 2 minutes

Yield: 6 servings
Preparation time: 2 hours

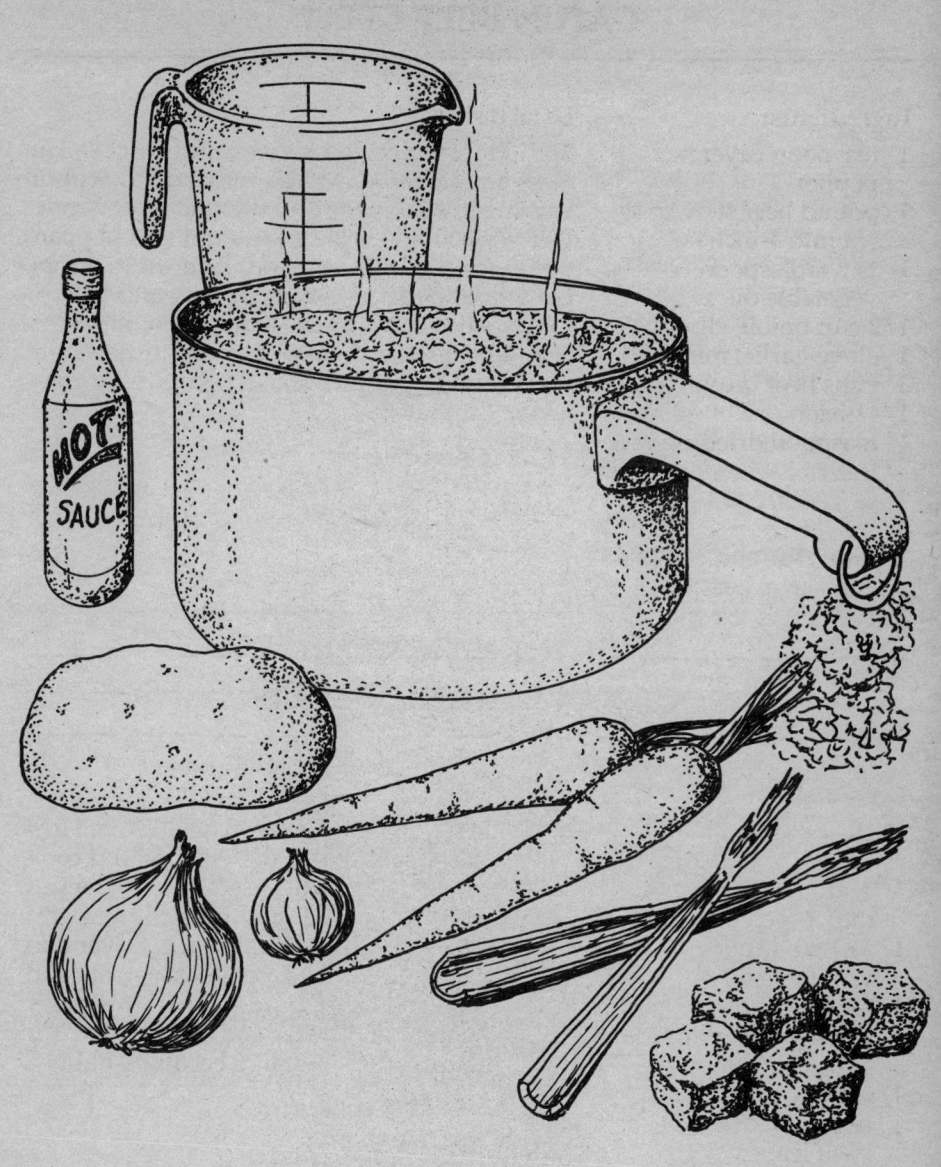

CAJUN CHILI

Ingredients:

1   pound lean ground beef
1/2 cup onion, chopped
2   (16 -ounce) cans
    kidney beans, reserve
    liquid
1   cup beef broth
2   teaspoons chili powder
1   teaspoon hot pepper
    flakes
1   teaspoon hot sauce
1   teaspoon black pepper
1/2 teaspoon ground
    ginger
1   teaspoon garlic powder

Directions:

Combine ground beef and onion in a medium-sized skillet. Cook until tender, about 5 minutes. Drain. Place in a large saucepan. Add beans, bean liquid, beef broth, chili powder, pepper flakes, hot sauce, black pepper, ginger and garlic powder. Cover and simmer for 2 hours.

Yield: 6 servings
Preparation time: 2 1/2 hours

CHICKEN GUMBO

Ingredients:

1   pound chicken breast,
    cut into 1-inch pieces
1/2 teaspoon pepper
    flakes
1/4 cup vegetable oil
1/4 cup all-purpose flour
1/4 cup onion, chopped
1/4 cup green pepper,
    chopped
1   cup celery, chopped
1   teaspoon garlic
    powder
2   quarts hot water
1   cup chicken broth
2   tablespoons filé
    powder (optional)
2   cups cooked rice

Directions:

Sprinkle chicken with red pepper flakes. Heat oil in a large saucepan. Add chicken and brown. Remove chicken. Add flour to oil and stir constantly until mixture becomes darker, about 5 minutes. Remove from heat. Add onion, green pepper, celery and garlic powder. Mix well. Return to heat and let simmer for 10 minutes. Gradually add water, chicken broth and chicken and bring to a boil. Reduce heat and cover; simmer for 1 hour. Remove from heat and stir in filé. Serve over cooked rice.

Yield: 6 servings
Preparation time: 2 hours

CHICKEN SOUP

Ingredients:

4 cups chicken broth
2 cups cooked chicken
1 cup celery, chopped
1/2 cup carrots, chopped
2 cups cooked rice
2 teaspoons cayenne pepper
1 teaspoon garlic powder
1 teaspoon salt
1/2 teaspoon black pepper
1 teaspoon dried parsley

Directions:

Combine chicken broth, chicken, celery and carrots in a large saucepan. Heat until boiling. Reduce heat, cover and simmer for 10 minutes. Add rice, cayenne pepper, garlic powder, salt, black pepper and parsley. Cover and simmer for 30 minutes.

Yield: 6 servings
Preparation time: 1 hour

CHICKEN SPINACH GUMBO

Ingredients:

2 (10-ounce) packages leaf spinach, thawed
4 tablespoons margarine
1/2 cup onion, chopped
1/2 cup green pepper
1 clove garlic, minced
2 tablespoons flour
4 cups chicken broth
1 (16-ounce) can stewed tomatoes
2 tablespoons fresh parsley
1 bay leaf
1/2 teaspoon dried thyme
1 pound boneless chicken breast, cut into 1 inch strips
2 teaspoon Worcestershire sauce

Directions:

Cook spinach according to package directions. Melt margarine in a large saucepan. Add onion, green pepper and garlic; cook until tender. Add flour. Mix well. Whisk in chicken broth, stirring constantly until mixture begins to thicken. Add spinach, tomatoes, parsley, bay leaf and thyme. Mix well. Add chicken. Cover and cook on medium heat for 30 minutes or until chicken is thoroughly cooked. Remove bay leaf. Add Worcestershire sauce. Serve over rice or separately.

Yield: 4 servings
Preparation time: 1 hour

HAM AND SPINACH GUMBO

Ingredients:

2 (10-ounce) packages
   leaf spinach, thawed
4 tablespoons margarine
1/2 cup onion, chopped
1/2 cup green pepper
1 clove garlic, minced
2 tablespoons flour
4 cups chicken broth
1 (16-ounce) can stewed
   tomatoes
2 tablespoons fresh
   parsley
1 bay leaf
1/2 teaspoon dried
   thyme
1 pound cooked ham,
   sliced 1/2-inch thick
2 teaspoon
   Worcestershire sauce

Directions:

Cook spinach according to package directions. Melt margarine in a large saucepan. Add onion, green pepper and garlic. Cook until tender. Add flour. Mix well. Whisk in chicken broth, stirring constantly, until mixture begins to thicken. Add spinach, tomatoes, parsley, bay leaf and thyme. Mix well. Lay ham on top of gumbo. Cover and cook on medium heat for 20 minutes or until ham is thoroughly heated. Remove bay leaf. Add Worcestershire sauce. Serve over rice or separately.

Yield: 4 servings
Preparation time: 1 hour

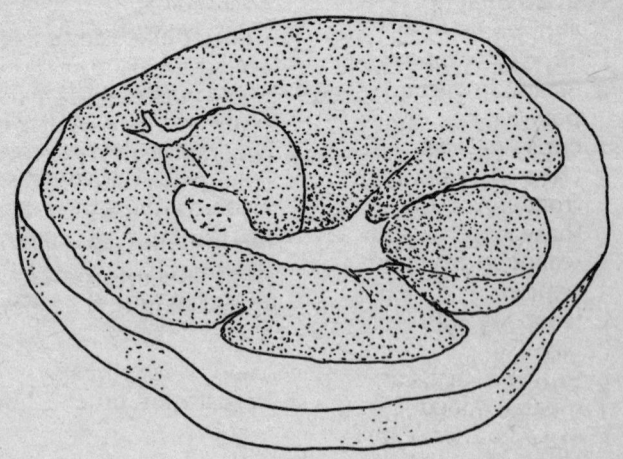

SEAFOOD GUMBO

Ingredients:

1/4 cup vegetable oil
1/4 cup all-purpose flour
1/4 cup onion, chopped
1/4 cup green pepper, chopped
1 cup celery, chopped
1 teaspoon garlic powder
6 cups hot water
1 (10-ounce) package frozen broccoli, thawed
1 teaspoon cayenne pepper
1 teaspoon salt
1 bay leaf
1 (6 1/2-ounce) can crab meat, drained
1 (6 1/2-ounce) can clams, drained
1 (6 1/2-ounce) can shrimp, drained
2 cups cooked rice

Directions:

Heat oil in a large saucepan. Add flour to oil and stir constantly until mixture becomes darker, about 5 minutes. Remove from heat. Add onion, green pepper and garlic powder. Mix well. Return to heat and let simmer for 10 minutes. Gradually add water, broccoli, cayenne pepper, salt and bay leaf and bring to a boil. Reduce heat and cover; simmer for 1 hour. Remove bay leaf. Add crab meat, clams and shrimp and simmer for 5 minutes or until seafood is thoroughly heated. Serve over cooked rice.

Yield: 6 servings
Preparation time: 2 hours

SHRIMP GUMBO

Ingredients:

1 pound fresh or frozen shrimp, shells reviewed
1/4 cup vegetable oil
1/4 cup all-purpose flour
1/4 cup onion, chopped
1/4 cup green pepper, chopped
1 teaspoon garlic powder
6 cups hot water
1 (10-ounce) package frozen okra, thawed
1 teaspoon cayenne pepper
1 teaspoon salt
1 bay leaf
2 cups cooked rice

Directions:

Thaw shrimp if using frozen. Clean and devein shrimp. Heat oil in a large saucepan. Add flour to oil and stir constantly until mixture becomes a dark red, about 5 minutes. Remove from heat. Add onion, green pepper and garlic powder. Mix well. Return to heat and let simmer for 10 minutes. Gradually add water, okra, cayenne pepper, salt and bay leaf and bring to a boil. Reduce heat and cover; simmer for 1 hour. Remove bay leaf. Add shrimp and simmer for 5 minutes or until shrimp is pink. Serve over cooked rice.

Yield: 6 servings
Preparation time: 2 hours

SHRIMP, CRAB MEAT AND VEGETABLE BISQUE

Ingredients:

1/4 cup plus 2 tablespoons vegetable oil
1 (10-ounce) package broccoli, thawed
1 (10-ounce) package frozen cauliflower, thawed
1/4 cup onions, chopped
1/4 cup red pepper, chopped
1/4 cup celery, chopped
1/4 cup mushrooms, sliced
1 teaspoon garlic powder
1/2 teaspoon cayenne powder
1 teaspoon black pepper
1/4 cup flour
4 cups vegetable stock or chicken stock
1 (6 1/2-ounce) can crab meat, drained
1 (6 1/2-ounce) can shrimp, drained

Directions:

Heat oil in a medium-sized skillet. Add broccoli and cauliflower. Cook until browned, about 4 minutes. Add onion, red pepper, celery and mushrooms; cook until tender. Sprinkle garlic powder, cayenne pepper and black pepper over vegetables. Mix well. Add 2 tablespoons reserved oil. Whisk in flour. Cook, stirring constantly for 2 minutes. Slowly add broth. Bring to a boil; boil for 3 minutes. Reduce heat and simmer for 10 minutes, stirring occasionally. Add crab meat and shrimp and simmer for 10 minutes. Serve immediately.

Yield: 6 servings
Preparation time: 45 minutes

TURKEY GUMBO

Ingredients:

1 pound turkey breast, cut into 1-inch pieces
1/2 teaspoon pepper flakes
1/4 cup vegetable oil
1/4 cup all-purpose flour
1/4 cup onion, chopped
1/4 cup green pepper, chopped
1 cup celery, chopped
1 teaspoon garlic powder
2 quarts hot water
1 cup chicken broth
2 tablespoons filé powder (optional)
2 cups cooked rice

Directions:

Sprinkle turkey with red pepper flakes. Heat oil in a large saucepan. Add turkey and brown. Remove turkey. Add flour to oil and stir constantly until mixture becomes dark, about 5 minutes. Remove from heat. Add onion, green pepper, celery and garlic powder. Mix well. Return to heat and let simmer for 10 minutes. Gradually add water, chicken broth and turkey and bring to a boil. Reduce heat and cover. Simmer for 1 hour. Remove from heat and stir in filé. Serve over cooked rice.

Yield: 6 servings
Preparation time: 2 hours

BARBECUED CHICKEN BREASTS

Ingredients:

1 tablespoon margarine
1/4 cup onion, chopped
1 clove garlic, minced
1 cup catsup
2 teaspoons honey
1/4 cup vinegar
2 teaspoons hot sauce
1 teaspoon cayenne pepper
1/2 teaspoon sage
1 teaspoon black pepper
1 teaspoon onion powder
1 pound boneless chicken breasts

Directions:

Melt margarine in a medium-sized skillet. Add onion and garlic and cook until tender. Add catsup, honey, vinegar, hot sauce, cayenne pepper, sage, black pepper and onion powder and heat thoroughly. Preheat oven to 350°F. Place chicken breasts in a large roasting pan. Brush with a layer of sauce. Bake for 20 minutes. Turn breasts, brush with sauce and bake 20 minutes. Let cool 5 minutes.

Yield: 4 servings
Preparation time: 1 hour

BARBECUED RIBS

Ingredients:

2 pounds pork ribs
1 tablespoon margarine
1/4 cup onion, chopped
1 clove garlic, minced
1 cup catsup
2 teaspoons brown
   sugar
1/4 cup vinegar
2 teaspoons hot sauce
1 teaspoon cayenne
   pepper
1/2 teaspoon cumin
1 teaspoon black pepper
1 teaspoon onion
   powder

Directions:

Boil ribs for 20 minutes in a large saucepan. Melt margarine in a medium-sized skillet. Add onion and garlic and cook until tender. Add catsup, brown sugar, vinegar, hot sauce, cayenne pepper, cumin, black pepper and onion pepper and heat thoroughly. Preheat oven to 350°F. Place ribs in a large roasting pan. Brush with a layer of sauce. Bake for 15 minutes. Turn ribs, brush with sauce and bake 10 minutes. Let cool 5 minutes.

Yield: 4 servings
Preparation time: 1 hour

CAJUN FRIED CHICKEN

Ingredients:

1 (3-pound) frying
   chicken, cut into 8
   pieces
1 teaspoon red pepper
   flakes, crushed
1 teaspoon salt
1/2 teaspoon white
   pepper
1/2 teaspoon black
   pepper
1/4 teaspoon cayenne
   pepper
1 1/2 cups flour
1/2 cup bread crumbs
2 eggs
1 1/2 cups milk
Vegetable oil for frying

Directions:

Remove excess fat from chicken. Combine red pepper flakes, salt, white pepper, black pepper, and cayenne pepper in a small bowl. Sprinkle over chicken and firmly rub in. Place flour and bread crumbs on a large flat plate. Beat eggs thoroughly and mix with milk. Half fill a large heavy skillet with oil. Heat to 375°F. (this will take 20 minutes). Once hot, coat chicken with flour, a few pieces at a time, dip in egg mixture and coat with flour a second time. Place in single layer in skillet. Cook for 8 minutes, turn and cook an additional 8 minutes, or until chicken is golden brown. Repeat using all chicken pieces.

Yield: 4 servings
Preparation time: 1 hour

CAJUN BAKED FISH

Ingredients:

1 teaspoon dried chervil
1/2 teaspoon cayenne
 pepper
1/2 teaspoon black
 pepper
2 tablespoons lemon
 juice
4 (1/2-inch thick) cod
 fillets, or trout, red
 snapper, redfish, bass
 or walleye

Directions:

Spray a baking dish with no-stick cooking spray. Preheat oven to 350°F. Combine chervil, cayenne pepper and black pepper in a small bowl. Add lemon juice and mix well. Place fish on baking dish and brush with lemon juice. Bake for 10 minutes. Turn over and brush with lemon juice and bake 15 more minutes, or until fish flakes easily when pierced with a fork.

Yield: 4 servings
Preparation time: 40 minutes

CAJUN ROAST BEEF

Ingredients:

2 medium onions,
 quartered
2 stalks celery, chopped
2 medium carrots, sliced
1 medium green pepper,
 sliced
1 cup mushrooms,
 whole
2 medium potatoes,
 quartered
1 teaspoon salt
1 teaspoon black pepper
1 teaspoon garlic
 powder
1 teaspoon cayenne
 pepper
1 (3-pound) boneless
 top round roast
1 teaspoon black pepper
3/4 cup beer

Directions:

Combine onions, celery, carrots, green pepper, mushrooms and potatoes in a medium-sized mixing bowl. Mix well. To this add salt, black pepper, garlic powder and cayenne pepper. Toss well. Place roast in a large roasting pan, fat side up. Sprinkle with black pepper. Pour beer over roast. Add vegetables. Cook uncovered for 3 hours or until a meat thermometer reads 160°F. Serve immediately, with vegetables.

Yield: 6 servings
Preparation time: 3 1/2 hours

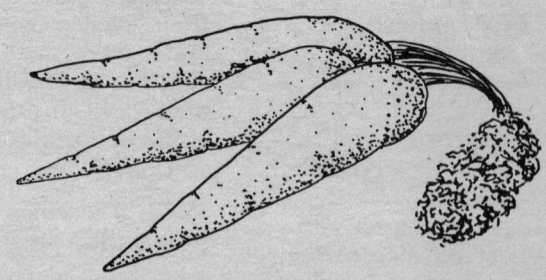

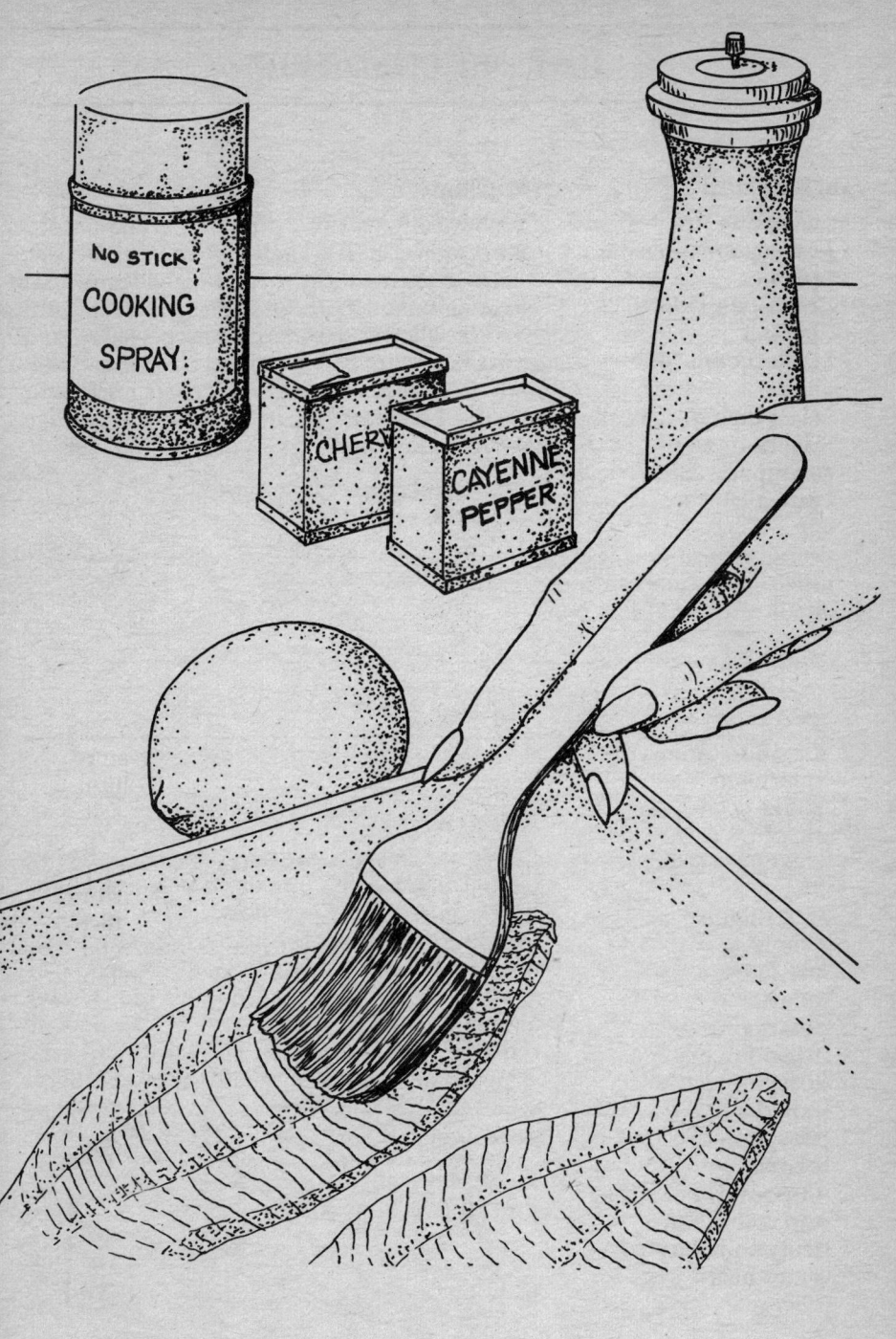

CAJUN SPICED CATFISH

Ingredients:

1   teaspoon salt
1   teaspoon cayenne
    pepper
1   teaspoon garlic
    powder
1   teaspoon white
    pepper
1   teaspoon dried parsley
1   teaspoon sage
2   cups flour
1/2 cup milk
1   egg
1   pound fresh fillets, cut
    into 2-inch squares
Vegetable oil for frying

Directions:

Combine salt, cayenne pepper, garlic powder, white pepper, parsley and sage in a small bowl. Combine flour and spice mixture on a large flat plate. Combine milk and egg in a medium-sized bowl. Mix well. Heat 3 inches of oil in a large skillet to 350°F. Put fillets in flour mixture and then egg mixture and return to flour mixture. Shake off excess. Place in oil. Cook fish until golden brown. Drain on paper towels.

Yield: 6 servings
Preparation: 40 minutes

CHICKEN FAJITAS

Ingredients:

2   tablespoons vegetable
    oil
1   pound boneless
    chicken breast, cut
    into 1-inch pieces
1   teaspoon paprika
1/2 teaspoon cayenne
    pepper
1/2 teaspoon cumin
3/4 teaspoon chili powder
1/2 teaspoon black pepper
1   tablespoon lemon juice
2   medium onions, sliced
2   medium green
    peppers, julienned
2   medium red peppers,
    julienned

Directions:

Combine chicken strips, paprika, cayenne pepper, cumin, chili powder, black pepper and lemon juice in a large bowl. Toss lightly to thoroughly coat. Cover and refrigerate for 30 minutes. Heat 1 tablespoon oil in a medium-sized skillet. Add chicken and cook until tender, about 8 minutes. Remove chicken. Add remaining oil, onions, green peppers and red peppers and cook until tender. Remove. Serve with warm tortillas, shredded cheese, salsa and guacamole.

Yield: 4 servings
Preparation time: 1 hour

PAN-FRIED SEASONED CHICKEN

Ingredients:
1/2 cup margarine,
   melted
1 pound boneless
   chicken breast
1 teaspoon cayenne
   pepper
1 teaspoon black pepper
1/2 teaspoon salt
1/4 teaspoon white
   pepper

Directions:
Spray a griddle or aluminum skillet with no-stick cooking spray. Heat a griddle or large aluminum skillet to 350°F. Pour melted margarine into a skillet. Combine cayenne pepper, black pepper, salt and white pepper in a small bowl. Sprinkle chicken with pepper mixture. Place chicken 2 pieces at a time in skillet. Cook each side for 5 minutes. Chicken should be golden brown. Repeat with remaining chicken.

Yield: 4 servings
Preparation time: 30 minutes

CAJUN SEASONED PORK CHOPS

Ingredients:

4 (1 1/2-inch thick) pork chops
2 cups Peppery Rice (page 58)
1 egg, beaten
1 cup flour
1 teaspoon cayenne pepper
1 teaspoon onion powder
1/2 teaspoon black pepper
1/2 teaspoon sage
1/2 teaspoon dried thyme leaves

Directions:

Preheat oven to 400°F. Spray a baking sheet with no-stick cooking spray. Prepare pork chops by cutting in horizontally to the bone. Stuff each with 1/2 cup peppery rice. Place egg in a medium-sized shallow dish. Combine cayenne pepper, onion powder, black pepper, sage and thyme in a large shallow dish. Mix well. Dip pork chops in egg mixture and then flour mixture. Place on baking sheet. Bake for 1 hour, or until pork chops are thoroughly cooked.

Yield: 4 servings
Preparation time: 1 1/2 hour

PEPPERED BURGERS

Ingredients:

1 pound ground beef
1 teaspoon onion powder
1 teaspoon red pepper flakes
1/2 teaspoon cumin
1 teaspoon black pepper
1/2 teaspoon garlic powder

Directions:

Preheat oven to broil. Spray a broiler pan with no-stick cooking spray. Combine ground beef, onion powder, pepper flakes, cumin, black pepper and garlic powder in a medium-sized bowl. Mix well. Shape into 4 patties. Place on broiler pan. Broil for 5 minutes on each side. Serve on a burger bun.

Yield: 4 burgers
Preparation time: 20 minutes

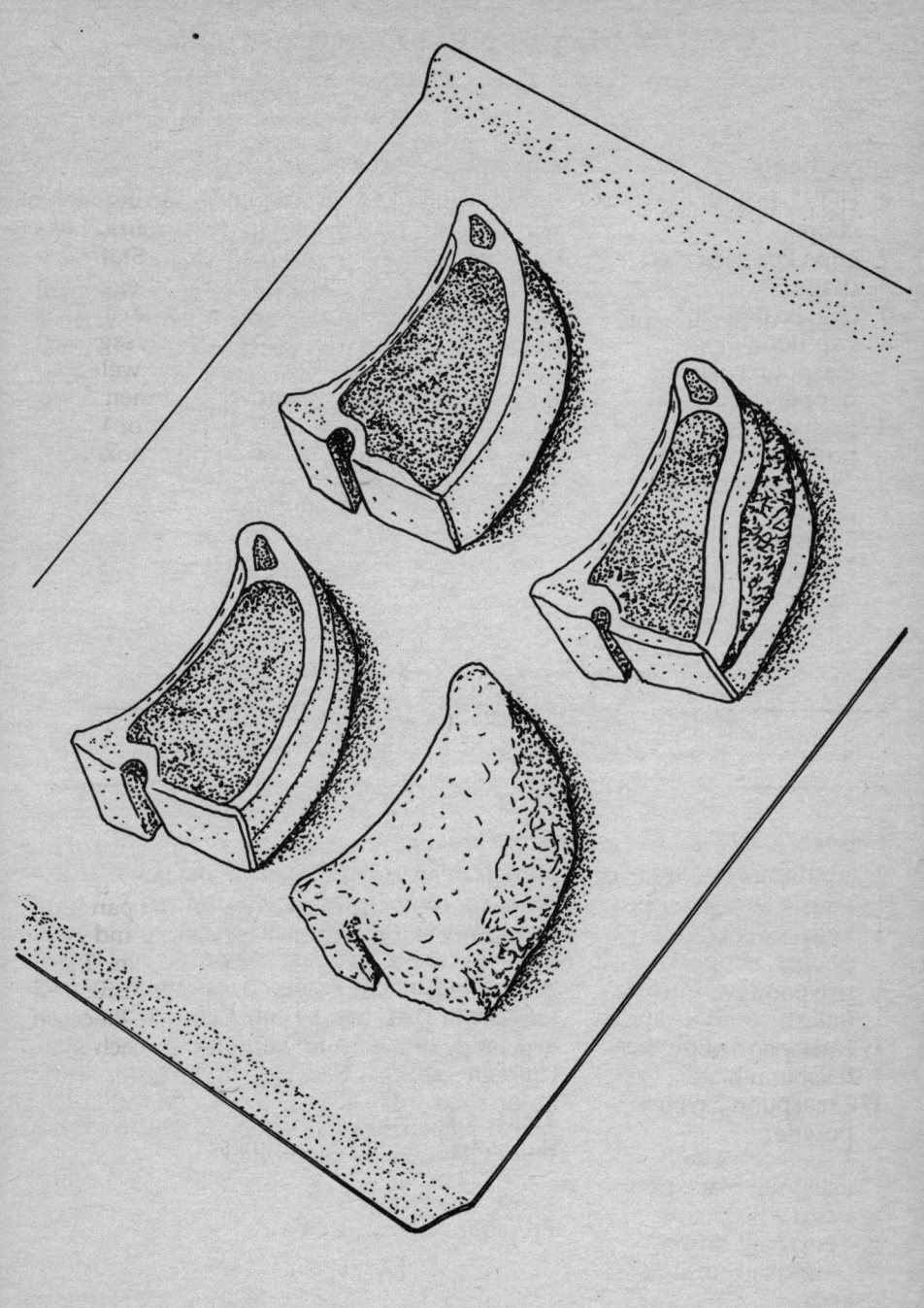

PAN-FRIED SNAPPER

Ingredients:
1/2 cup margarine, melted
1 teaspoon cayenne pepper
1 teaspoon black pepper
1/2 teaspoon salt
1/4 teaspoon chervil
4 (4 1/2-ounce) red snapper fillets

Directions:
Spray an aluminum skillet with no-stick cooking spray and heat to 350°F. Pour melted margarine into a large pan. Combine cayenne pepper, black pepper, salt and white pepper in a small bowl. Sprinkle red snapper with pepper mixture. Place red snapper in skillet, 2 at a time. Cook each side for 5 minutes. Red snapper should be golden brown. Repeat with remaining fillets.

Yield: 4 servings
Preparation time: 30 minutes

SPICY MEAT LOAF

Ingredients:
2 tablespoons margarine
1/2 cup onion, chopped
1/4 cup sweet red pepper, chopped
1 clove garlic, minced
1 tablespoon hot sauce
1 teaspoon red pepper flakes
1/2 teaspoon cayenne pepper
1/2 teaspoon cumin
1 teaspoon black pepper
1/4 cup catsup
1/4 cup chili sauce
2 pounds ground beef
2 eggs
1/2 cup bread crumbs

Directions:
Preheat oven to 350°F. Spray a loaf pan with no-stick cooking spray. Melt margarine in a medium-sized skillet. Add onion, red pepper, garlic, hot sauce, pepper flakes, cayenne pepper, cumin and black pepper. Sauté until mixture sticks to the pan. Scrape pan. Remove from heat and add catsup and chili sauce. Let cool. Combine ground beef, egg, bread crumbs and onion mixture in a large bowl. Mix well. Place into a loaf pan. Bake for 1 hour. Cool 10 minutes. Place on a serving platter.

Yield: 6 servings
Preparation time: 2 hours

SPICY STEW

Ingredients:

3   tablespoons flour
1   teaspoon black pepper
1/2 teaspoon cayenne pepper
1/2 teaspoon garlic powder
1/2 teaspoon cumin
1   pound beef stew meat, cut into 1-inch cubes
1   tablespoon vegetable oil
1   medium onion, chopped in large chunks
1   teaspoon dried thyme leaves
3   cups beef broth
1   teaspoon hot sauce
2   medium potatoes, cubed
3   stalks celery, sliced
3   carrots, sliced

Directions:

Combine flour, black pepper, cayenne pepper, garlic powder and cumin in a plastic bag. Add meat cubes a few at a time, shaking to coat. Heat oil in a large saucepan. Add meat and brown. Add onion and thyme. Cook until onion is tender. Add beef broth and hot sauce and bring to a boil. Reduce heat and add potatoes, celery and carrots. Cover and simmer for 1 1/2 hours.

Yield: 6 servings
Preparation time: 2 hours

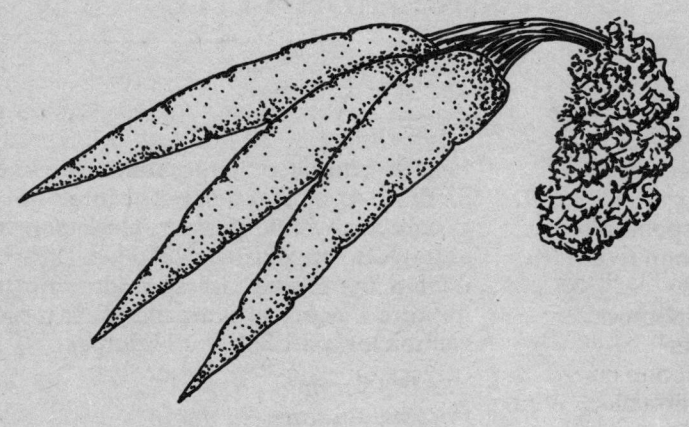

ROASTED PORK

Ingredients:

2 medium onions, quartered
1 medium red pepper, sliced
1 medium green pepper, sliced
1 cup mushrooms, whole
2 medium potatoes, quartered
1 teaspoon salt
2 teaspoons black pepper
1 teaspoon garlic powder
1 teaspoon cayenne pepper
1/4 teaspoon white pepper
1 (4-pound) boneless pork loin roast
1/2 cup water

Directions:

Combine onions, red pepper, green pepper, mushrooms and potatoes in a medium-sized mixing bowl. Mix well. To this add salt, black pepper, garlic powder, cayenne pepper and white pepper. Toss well. Place roast in a large roasting pan, fat side up. Sprinkle with black pepper. Pour water over roast. Add vegetables. Cook uncovered for 3 hours or until a meat thermometer reads 160°F. Increase heat to 425°F. Cook 15 minutes or until meat is no longer pink.

Yield: 6 servings
Preparation time: 3 1/2 hours

STEAK CAJUN-STYLE

Ingredients:

1/2 cup margarine, melted
1 teaspoon cayenne pepper
1 teaspoon black pepper
1/2 teaspoon salt
1/4 teaspoon white pepper
4 rib eye steaks

Directions:

Heat a griddle or large aluminum skillet to 350°F. Pour melted margarine into a large pan. Combine cayenne pepper, black pepper, salt and white pepper in a small bowl. Dip steaks in melted margarine and sprinkle with pepper mixture. Place steaks in skillet, 2 at a time. Cook each side for 3 1/2 minutes. Repeat.

Yield: 4 servings
Preparation time: 30 minutes

SEAFOOD CREOLE

Ingredients:

2 tablespoons margarine
1/4 cup onion, chopped
1/4 cup red pepper, chopped
1 clove garlic
1 (16-ounce) can tomatoes
1 teaspoon basil
1/2 teaspoon cayenne pepper
1/2 teaspoon salt
1/4 teaspoon white pepper
3 teaspoons cornstarch
2 tablespoons cold water
1/2 pound fresh shrimp or frozen shrimp, thawed
1/2 pound fresh crab meat or frozen, thawed
2 cups Peppery Rice (page 58)

Directions:

Melt margarine in a medium-sized skillet. Add onion, red pepper and garlic. Cook until tender, about 4 minutes. Add tomatoes, basil, cayenne pepper, salt and white pepper. Cover, reduce heat and simmer for 10 minutes. Combine cornstarch and water in a small bowl. Mix well. Add to tomato mixture. Stir until bubbly. Add shrimp and crab meat and heat to boiling. Reduce heat, cover and simmer for 10 minutes or until seafood is thoroughly cooked. Serve on top of rice.

Yield: 4 servings
Preparation time: 40 minutes

TURKEY BURGERS

Ingredients:

1 pound ground turkey
1 teaspoon garlic powder
1 teaspoon cayenne pepper
1/2 teaspoon cumin
1 teaspoon black pepper

Directions:

Preheat oven to broil. Spray a broiler pan with no-stick cooking spray. Combine ground turkey, garlic powder, cayenne pepper, cumin and black pepper in a medium-sized bowl. Mix well. Shape into 4 patties. Place on broiler pan. Broil for 5 minutes on each side. Serve on a burger bun.

Yield: 4 burgers
Preparation time: 20 minutes

SWEET CAJUN SHRIMP

Ingredients:

1   cup catsup
1   tablespoon honey
1   tablespoon brown
    sugar
2   tablespoons vinegar
2   teaspoons hot sauce
1   teaspoon cayenne
    pepper
1/2 teaspoon thyme
1   teaspoon black pepper
1   teaspoon onion
    powder
1   pound cleaned fresh
    shrimp, or frozen
    shrimp thawed

Directions:

Combine catsup, honey, brown sugar, vinegar, hot sauce, cayenne pepper, thyme, black pepper and onion powder in a medium saucepan. Heat thoroughly. Cook shrimp in boiling water for 5 minutes or until shrimp turns pink. Brush sauce over shrimp and serve over rice. Serve with leftover sauce.

Yield: 4 servings
Preparation time: 30 minutes

TURKEY CURRY

Ingredients:

2 tablespoons vegetable oil
1 pound boneless turkey breast slices
1/4 cup chicken broth
2 tablespoons onion, chopped
3/4 cup sour cream
2 tablespoons curry powder
1 teaspoon cayenne powder
1/2 teaspoon cumin
1/2 teaspoon ginger
1/2 teaspoon ground tumeric
1/2 teaspoon white pepper
1/2 teaspoon parsley
1/2 teaspoon ground coriander
2 cups Peppery Rice (page 58)

Directions:

Heat oil in a medium-sized skillet. Add turkey slices and brown on both sides, about 10 minutes. Drain fat from skillet and add chicken broth and onion. Reduce heat, cover and simmer for 10 minutes, or until turkey is fully cooked. Remove turkey from skillet. Add sour cream, curry powder, cayenne pepper, cumin, ginger, tumeric, pepper, parsley and coriander. Mix well and heat thoroughly. Place turkey over rice; pour sauce over turkey.

Yield: 4 servings
Preparation time: 45 minutes

BANANA WALNUT MUFFINS

Ingredients:

3   large bananas
1/2 cup sugar
1/2 cup brown sugar
2   eggs
1/2 cup margarine, melted
1   cup all-purpose flour
1   cup whole wheat flour
1   1/2 teaspoons baking
    soda
3   tablespoons buttermilk
1/4 cup walnuts, chopped

Directions:

Preheat oven to 300°F. Spray 12-muffin tin with no-stick cooking spray. Mash bananas in a medium-sized mixing bowl. Add sugar, brown sugar and eggs. Mix well. Add butter. Stir in flour, whole wheat flour and soda. Add buttermilk and walnuts. Mix until just moistened. Spoon into muffin tin. Bake until muffins are browned and done, about 20 minutes.

Yield: 12 muffins
Preparation time: 40 minutes

CAJUN BISCUITS

Ingredients:

2   cups flour
2   teaspoons sugar
1/2 teaspoon salt
1/4 teaspoon baking
    powder
1   teaspoon dried basil
1   teaspoon dried parsley
1/4 cup shortening
1/3 cup milk
1/3 cup water

Directions:

Preheat oven to 450°F. Combine flour, sugar, salt, baking powder, basil and parsley in a medium-sized mixing bowl. Add shortening and mix with a pastry cutter until mixture resembles coarse crumbs. Make a well in the center of flour. Add milk and water. Mix well. Turn dough out onto a floured surface. Knead for 15 minutes, using more flour if necessary. Roll dough out to a 1/2-inch thickness. Cut dough with a 2-inch cookie cutter. Place on an ungreased cookie sheet. Pierce tops of biscuits with a fork. Bake for 20 minutes, or until lightly browned.

Yield: 16 servings
Preparation time: 50 minutes

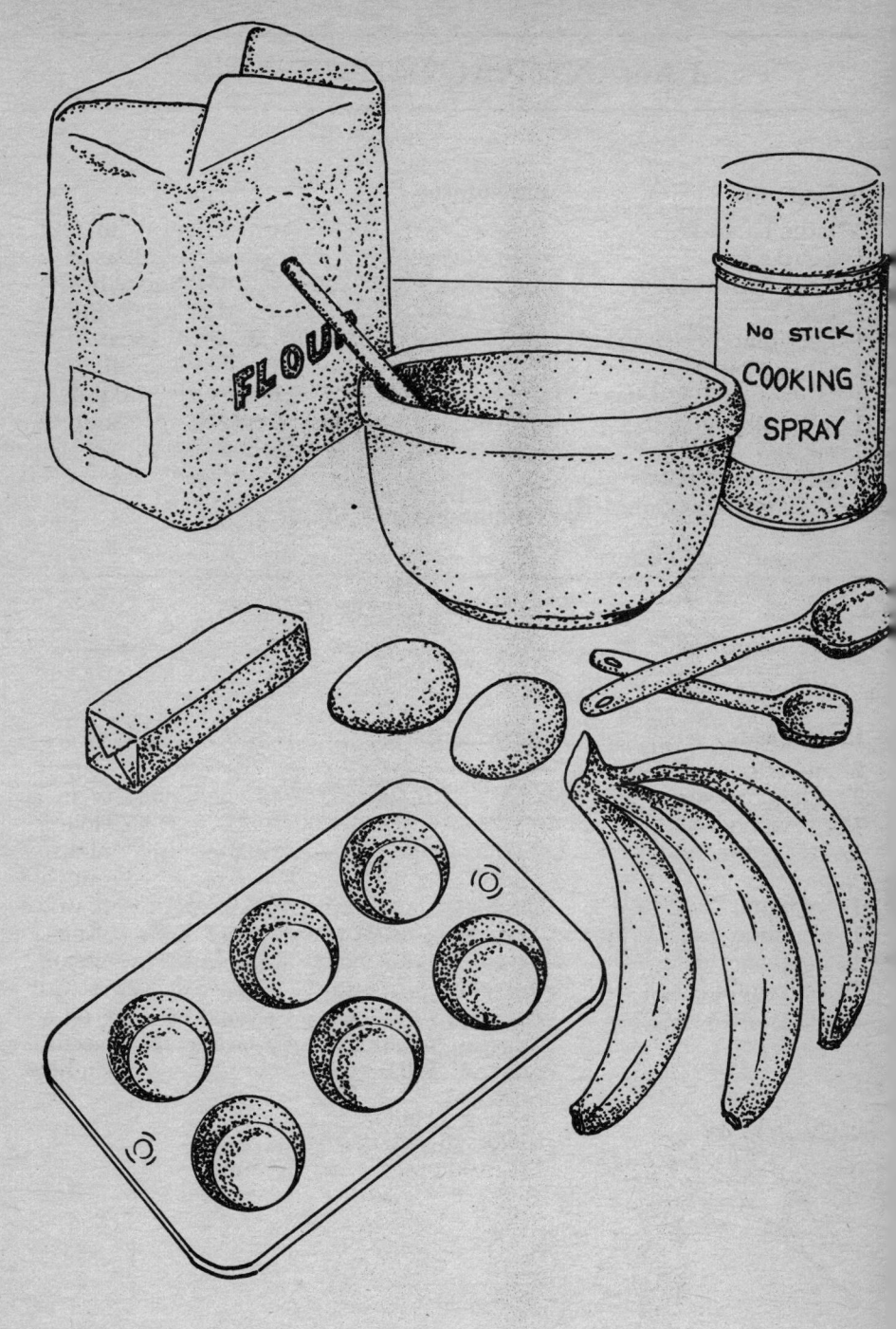

CAJUN MACARONI AND TUNA

Ingredients:

2   cups elbow macaroni, uncooked
1   (6 1/2-ounce) can tuna, drained
1/2 cup celery, chopped
1/2 cup sweet red pepper, chopped
1/4 cup vinegar
1   teaspoon onion salt
1   teaspoon dried basil
1/4 teaspoon cayenne pepper
1   teaspoon dry mustard
1/4 teaspoon white pepper
3/4 cup mayonnaise
2   hard boiled eggs, chopped

Directions:

Cook macaroni according to package directions. Drain and place in a large salad bowl. Add tuna, celery, and red pepper. Mix well. Combine vinegar, onion salt, basil, cayenne pepper, mustard and white pepper in a small bowl. Mix well. Pour over macaroni mixture and toss lightly to distribute. Add mayonnaise. Mix well. Garnish with chopped eggs. Cover and refrigerate for 30 minutes.

Yield: 6 servings
Preparation time: 1 hour

CAJUN SCRAMBLE

Ingredients:

2   tablespoons margarine
6   eggs
1   teaspoon chili powder
1   teaspoon hot sauce
1/4 cup milk

Directions:

Spray a medium-sized skillet with no-stick cooking spray. Melt margarine in skillet. Combine eggs, chili powder, hot sauce and milk in a medium-sized bowl. Mix well. Pour eggs in skillet. Cook until desired consistency. Serve immediately.

Yield: 2 servings
Preparation time: 20 minutes

CAJUN POACHED EGGS

Ingredients:

4   eggs
2   English muffins, split
    open
2   tablespoons margarine
2   tablespoons flour
1   cup milk
1   teaspoon dry mustard
1   teaspoon hot sauce
1/2 teaspoon chili
    powder
1/4 teaspoon white
    pepper

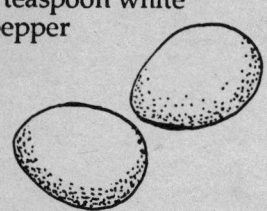

Directions:

Fill a medium-sized saucepan half way with water. Heat to just boiling. Break eggs one at a time in a custard dish and carefully slip into boiling water. Repeat. Cover and cook on low heat for 5 minutes or until desired hardness. Remove with a slotted spoon and place on English muffin half. Hold in a warm (110° F.) oven. Melt margarine in a medium-sized skillet. Add flour and mix well. Slowly add milk, mustard, hot sauce, chili powder and white pepper, stirring constantly until mixture thickens. Pour over eggs. Serve immediately.

Yield: 4 servings
Preparation time: 30 minutes

HERBY BISCUITS

Ingredients:

2   cups flour
2   teaspoons sugar
1/2 teaspoon salt
1/4 teaspoon baking
    powder
1   teaspoon dried parsley
1   teaspoon dried basil
1   teaspoon thyme leaves
1/4 cup shortening
1/3 cup milk
1/3 cup water

Directions:

Preheat oven to 450°F. Combine flour, sugar, salt, baking powder, parsley, basil and thyme in a medium-sized mixing bowl. Add shortening and mix with a pastry cutter until mixture resembles coarse crumbs. Make a well in the center of flour. Add milk and water. Mix well. Turn dough out onto a floured surface. Knead for 15 minutes, using more flour if necessary. Roll dough out to a 1/2-inch thickness. Cut dough with a 2-inch cookie cutter. Place on an a cookie sheet. Pierce tops of biscuits with a fork. Bake for 20 minutes or until lightly browned.

Yield: 16 servings
Preparation time: 50 minutes

CORN BREAD

Ingredients:

- 1 3/4 cup all-purpose flour
- 3/4 cup yellow cornmeal
- 1/3 cup sugar
- 4 teaspoons baking powder
- 1 teaspoon salt
- 1 1/3 cups milk
- 1/4 cup margarine, melted
- 1 beaten egg

Directions:

Spray a loaf pan with no-stick cooking spray. Combine flour, cornmeal, sugar, baking powder and salt in a large bowl; mix well. Combine milk, butter and egg in another bowl. Mix well. Add to dry ingredients. Mix until moistened. Pour into prepared loaf pan. Bake for 55 to 60 minutes or until golden brown. Remove from pan.

Yield: 1 loaf
Preparation time: 1 1/2 hours

CHEESE BISCUITS

Ingredients:

2 cups flour
2 teaspoons sugar
1/2 teaspoon salt
1/4 teaspoon baking
    powder
1/4 cup Cheddar cheese
1 tablespoon Jalapeño
    peppers, chopped
1/4 cup shortening
1/3 cup milk
1/3 cup water

Directions:

Preheat oven to 450°F. In a medium-sized mixing bowl, combine flour, sugar, salt, baking powder, cheese and Jalapeño peppers. Add shortening and mix with a pastry cutter until mixture resembles coarse crumbs. Make a well in the center of flour. Add milk and water. Mix well. Turn dough out onto a floured surface. Knead for 15 minutes, using more flour if necessary. Roll dough out to a 1/2-inch thickness. Cut dough with a 2-inch cookie cutter. Place on a cookie sheet. Pierce tops of biscuits with a fork. Bake for 20 minutes or until lightly browned.

Yield: 16 servings
Preparation time: 50 minutes

JALAPEÑO MUFFINS

Ingredients:

1 3/4 cups all-purpose
    flour
3/4 cup yellow cornmeal
1/3 cup sugar
4 teaspoons baking
    powder
1 teaspoon salt
1 1/3 cups milk
1/4 cup margarine,
    melted
1 beaten egg
3 tablespoons Jalapeño
    pepper, chopped

Directions:

Spray 12-muffin tin with no-stick cooking spray. Combine flour, cornmeal, sugar, baking powder and salt in a large bowl; mix well. Combine milk, margarine, egg and Jalapeño in another bowl. Mix well. Add to dry ingredients and mix until moistened. Pour into prepared muffin tin. Bake for 25 to 60 minutes or until golden brown. Remove from pan.

Yield: 1 loaf
Preparation time: 1 1/2 hours

OMELETTE CAJUN STYLE

Ingredients:
- 2 tablespoons margarine
- 1/4 cup onion, chopped
- 1/4 cup green pepper, chopped
- 1/4 cup mushrooms, chopped
- 1 medium tomato, chopped
- 6 eggs
- 1 teaspoon cayenne pepper
- 1/4 teaspoon white pepper
- 1/2 teaspoon cumin
- 1/4 cup milk

Directions:

Spray a large skillet with no-stick cooking spray. Melt margarine in skillet. Add onion, green pepper, mushrooms and tomato. Cook until tender, about 5 minutes. Combine eggs, cayenne pepper, white pepper, cumin and milk in a medium-sized bowl. Mix well. Pour over vegetable mixture. Cook about 30 seconds or until eggs begin to set. As soon as there is a base to the egg, use a spatula to pull uncooked eggs from outside the pan to the middle of pan. Continue, cooking until eggs are the desired consistency. Remove from pan. Serve immediately.

Yield: 2 servings
Preparation time: 20 minutes

SPICY TOMATO PASTA PRIMAVERA

Ingredients:
- 1/2 pound fettuccine, uncooked
- 2 medium tomatoes, chopped
- 1 tablespoon Jalapeño pepper, chopped
- 1 tablespoon olive oil
- 1 teaspoon garlic powder
- 1 teaspoon hot pepper flakes
- 1 teaspoon hot sauce

Directions:

Cook fettuccine according to package directions. Drain and set aside. Place tomatoes and Jalapeño peppers in a blender cup. Purée until almost smooth. Heat oil in a medium-sized skillet. Add tomato mixture, garlic powder, pepper flakes and hot sauce. Heat thoroughly. Pour over pasta.

Yield: 6 servings
Preparation time: 30 minutes

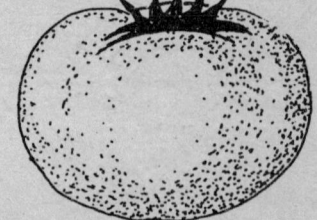

MILK

BROILED TOMATOES

Ingredients:

3 medium tomatoes, sliced into 1/4-inch slices
1 teaspoon dried parsley
1/2 teaspoon dried thyme leaves
1/2 teaspoon dried oregano leaves
1/2 teaspoon white pepper
1/4 teaspoon salt
1/4 cup Romano cheese, freshly grated

Directions:

Preheat oven to broil. Place tomato slices on broiler pan. Combine parsley, thyme, oregano, pepper and salt in a small bowl. Sprinkle over tomatoes, followed by cheese. Broil for 2 minutes or until cheese is melted. Serve immediately.

Yield: 6 servings
Preparation time: 20 minutes

CAJUN POTATO SKINS

Ingredients:

4 medium potatoes
1 teaspoon red pepper flakes
1 teaspoon cumin
1/2 teaspoon salt
1/4 teaspoon onion powder
1/4 cup Monterey Jack cheese, grated
2 tablespoons Jalapeño pepper, chopped

Directions:

Preheat oven to 350°F. Pierce each potato once with a fork. Bake for 1 hour or until potato is tender. Let cool for 10 minutes. Cut potatoes into 4 equal portions. Scoop out all but 1/4-inch pulp. Set pulp aside. (Use potato pulp for Cajun Potato Pancakes). Place potato skins on a baking dish. Combine red pepper flakes, cumin, salt and onion powder in a small bowl. Sprinkle over potato skins. Sprinkle with cheese and Jalapeño peppers. Bake for 10 minutes or until cheese is melted.

Yield: 16 potato skins
Preparation time: 1 1/2 hours

CAJUN FRIED VEGGIES

Ingredients:

3 cups all-purpose flour
1 teaspoon cayenne
   pepper
1/4 teaspoon filé powder
   (optional)
1 teaspoon garlic
   powder
1 tablespoon white
   pepper
1 teaspoon black pepper
1 teaspoon salt
1 egg
2 cups milk
2 tablespoons lemon
   juice
1 teaspoon onion salt
2 teaspoons sugar
2 large onions, sliced
   into 1/2-inch slices
2 cups whole
   mushrooms
2 cups broccoli
   flowerets
Vegetable oil for frying

Directions:

Combine flour, cayenne pepper, filé powder, garlic powder, white pepper, black pepper and salt in a medium-sized bowl. Mix well. Combine egg, milk, lemon juice, onion salt and sugar in a separate bowl. Mix well. Heat 2 inches of oil to 350°F. in a medium-sized skillet. Coat vegetables in flour mixture and then the milk mixture. Place back into flour; shake excess. Place in vegetable oil. Fry for 4 minutes or until golden brown. Remove with a slotted spoon. Drain on paper towels.

Yield: 8 servings
Preparation time: 30 minutes

BROILED ZUCCHINI

Ingredients:

2 medium zucchini,
   sliced
1 teaspoon dried parsley
1 teaspoon dried basil
1 teaspoon sweet
   paprika

Directions:

Preheat oven to broil. Place zucchini on a broiler pan. Sprinkle with parsley, basil and paprika. Broil for 2 minutes or zucchini is tender.

Yield: 4 servings
Preparation time: 15 minutes

CAJUN STUFFED ZUCCHINI

Ingredients:

2 small zucchini, sliced in half horizontally
1 cup carrots, diced
1 cup mushrooms, sliced
1/2 cup green pepper, chopped
1 medium tomato, chopped
1 teaspoon cayenne pepper
1 teaspoon paprika
1/2 teaspoon white pepper
1/2 teaspoon onion powder
1/2 teaspoon garlic powder

Directions:

Half fill a medium-sized saucepan with water. Heat until boiling. Add zucchini and cook until almost tender. Cut out the pulp from zucchini and chop pulp into bite-sized pieces. Place zucchini skins on a serving platter. Fill a medium-sized saucepan with 4-inches of water. Heat until boiling. Add chopped zucchini, carrots, mushrooms and tomato. Cook until tender, about 5 minutes. Remove from pan and place in a mixing bowl. Combine cayenne pepper, paprika, white pepper, onion powder and garlic powder in a small bowl. Mix well. Add to vegetables. Mix well. Place 1/4 of vegetable mixture in zucchini skin. Serve immediately.

Yield: 4 servings
Preparation time: 30 minutes

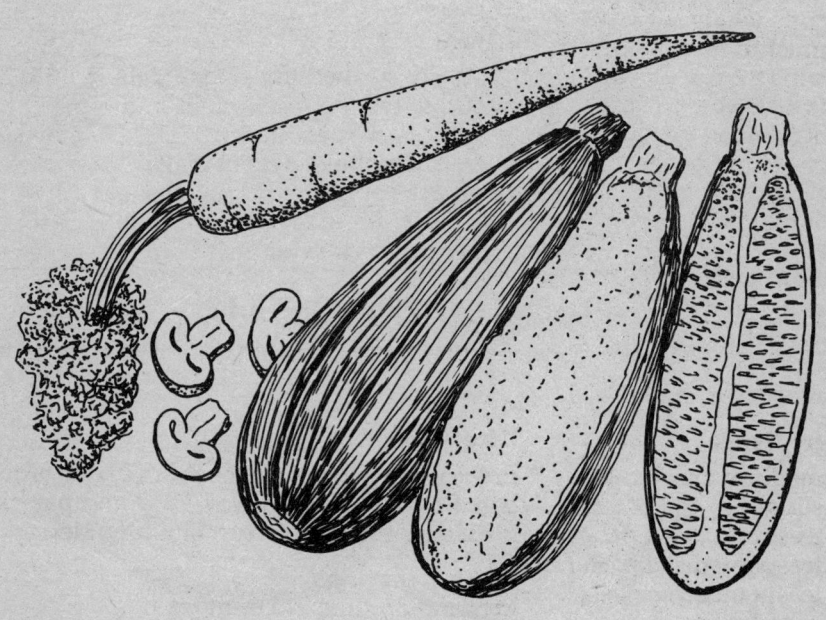

PEPPERY RICE

Ingredients:

2 cups brown rice
4 cups chicken broth
1/4 cup green onion, chopped
1/4 cup red peppers, chopped
1/2 teaspoon salt
1/4 teaspoon garlic powder
1/4 teaspoon cayenne pepper
1/4 teaspoon white pepper

Directions:

Place rice and chicken broth in a 3-quart saucepan. Bring to a boil. Reduce heat, cover and simmer for 20 minutes. Add onion, red peppers, salt, garlic powder, cayenne pepper and white pepper. Simmer an additional 20 minutes.

Yield: 6 servings
Preparation time: 1 hour

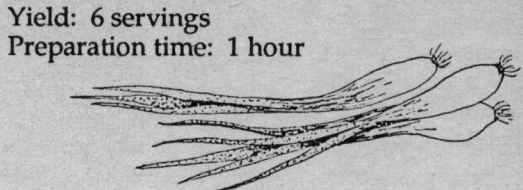

VEGETABLE STIR FRY

Ingredients:

1 tablespoon vegetable oil
1 cup mushrooms, sliced
1 cup sweet red pepper, sliced into 1/2-inch pieces
1 medium onion, thinly sliced
1 medium yellow squash, sliced
1 teaspoon red pepper flakes
1/2 teaspoon cayenne pepper
1/2 teaspoon black pepper
1/2 teaspoon garlic powder
1/4 teaspoon salt
2 cups Pepper Rice (page 58)

Directions:

Heat oil in a medium-sized skillet. Add mushrooms, red pepper, onion and squash. Cook until tender, about 5 minutes. Remove from heat. Combine pepper flakes, cayenne pepper, black pepper, garlic powder and salt in a small bowl. Sprinkle over vegetables. Mix well. Place rice in a serving dish. Pour vegetables over rice.

Yield: 4 servings
Preparation time: 30 minutes

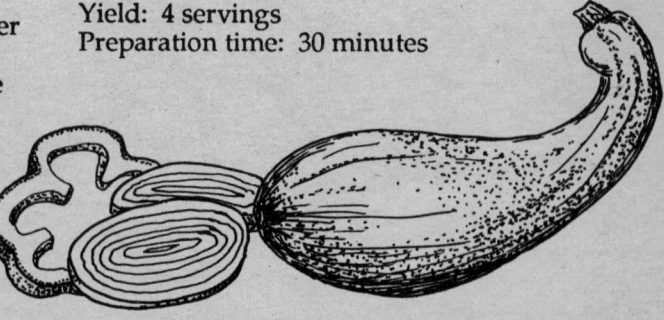

YAMS

Ingredients:

- 1 cup brown sugar
- 1/4 cup orange juice
- 1 orange, peeled and sectioned
- 2 tablespoons lemon juice
- 1/2 teaspoon ground nutmeg
- 1/2 teaspoon ground mace
- 2 pounds sweet potatoes, quartered
- 1/2 cup chopped walnuts
- 1 tablespoon margarine

Directions:

Preheat oven to 350°F. Spray a 2-quart casserole dish with no-stick cooking spray. Combine sugar, orange juice, orange sections, lemon juice, nutmeg and mace in a medium-sized mixing bowl. Add potatoes and walnuts. Place in a 2-quart casserole dish. Dot with margarine. Bake for 50 minutes or until tender. Spoon glaze over occasionally.

Yield: 8 servings
Preparation time: 1 1/4 hours

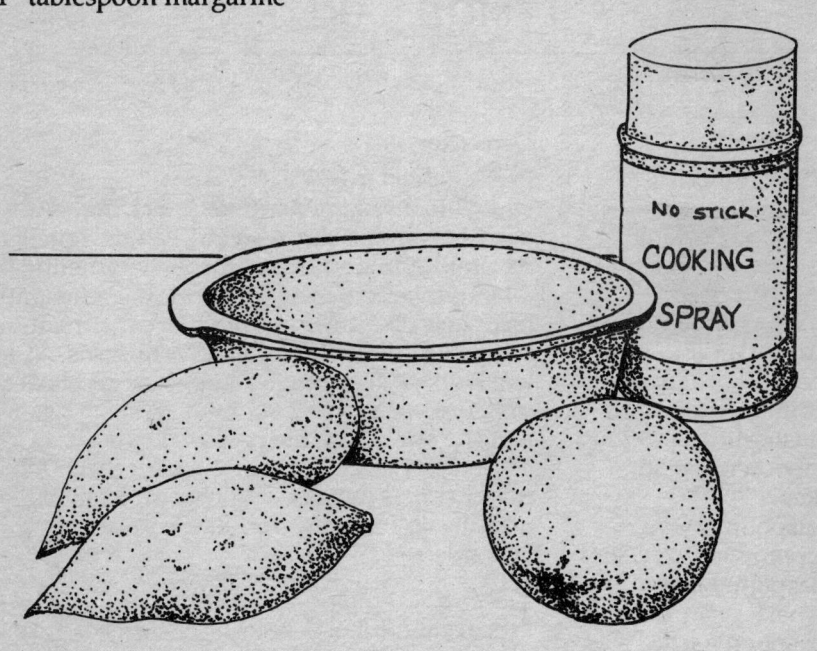

CINNAMON BREAD PUDDING

Ingredients:

4   eggs
3/4 cup sugar
1   teaspoon vanilla
1   1/2 teaspoon
    cinnamon
2   cups milk
2   tablespoons
    margarine, melted
1/2 cup raisins
4   cups very stale bread

Directions:

Spray a 8 x 1 1/2-inch baking dish with no-stick cooking spray. Preheat oven to 325°F. Place eggs in a medium-sized bowl. Beat until eggs are frothy (2 minutes on high with mixer or 4 minutes by hand). Add sugar, vanilla, cinnamon, margarine and milk. Mix well. Add raisins. Place bread cubes in baking dish. Pour milk mixture over bread. Bake for 45 minutes or until a knife inserted in comes out clean. Cool.

Yield: 6 servings
Preparation time: 1 hour

LEMON CAKE

Ingredients:

2   1/2 cups flour
1   1/2 cups sugar
3   teaspoons baking
    powder
1   teaspoon salt
1   cup and 2 tablespoons
    milk
2   tablespoons lemon
    juice
2/3 cup solid shortening
2   teaspoons lemon
    extract
4   eggs
1/2 cup pecans, crushed
2   cups coconut

Directions:

Preheat oven to 350°F. Grease and lightly flour a 13 x 9-inch baking pan (or 2, 9-inch round cake pans). Combine flour, sugar, baking powder, salt, milk, lemon juice, and solid shortening in a large mixing bowl. Beat on low speed until moistened (50 strokes by hand). Beat at medium speed for 2 minutes (200 strokes by hand). Add lemon extract and eggs and pecans and beat at medium speed for 2 minutes (200 strokes by hand). Pour batter into prepared pans. Bake for 45 minutes or until a toothpick inserted in the center comes out clean. Cool completely. Frost with basic frosting. Sprinkle coconut on top and sides.

Yield: 8 servings
Preparation time: 1 hour

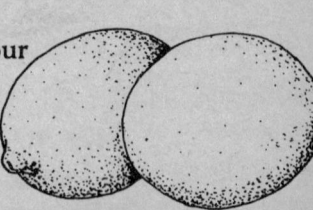

LIME PIE

Ingredients:

1 9-inch pie crust, unbaked
1 can sweetened condensed milk
1 tablespoon grated lime peel
1 tablespoon grated lemon peel
3/4 cup lime juice
2 egg yolks
2 egg whites
2 tablespoons sugar

Directions:

Preheat oven to 350°F. Bake pie crust for 15 minutes. Remove from oven and cool. Combine milk, lime and lemon peel, lime juice and egg yolks in a medium-sized mixing bowl. Beat on medium speed until mixture begins to thicken. Pour into pie shell. Place egg whites in a small mixing bowl and whip until soft peaks form. Add sugar slowly and beat until stiff peaks form. Place over lime mixture. Bake for 15 minutes or until meringue is lightly browned. Cool.

Yield: 1 9-inch pie
Preparation time: 45 minutes

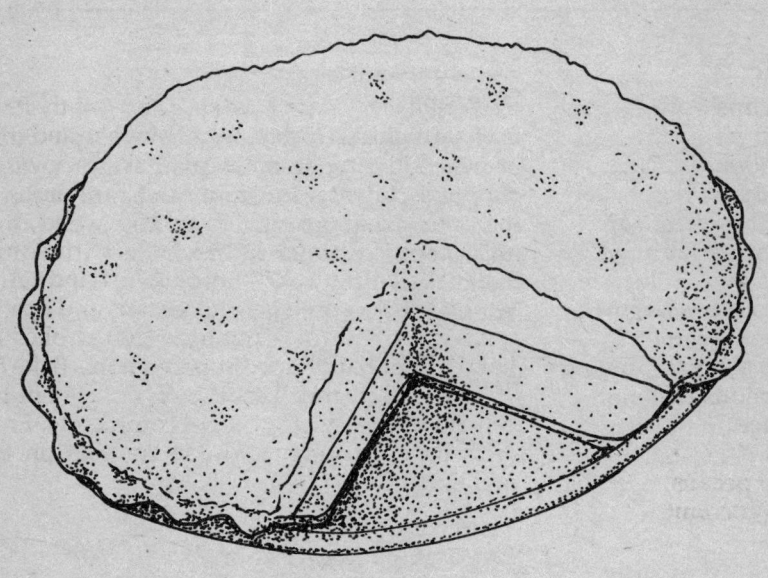

NUTTY RICE PUDDING

Ingredients:

2 cups milk
3/4 cup brown rice
1/4 cup margarine
3 beaten eggs
2 cups milk
1/2 cup brown sugar
1 teaspoon almond extract
1 teaspoon cinnamon
1 teaspoon nutmeg
1/2 cup pecans, chopped

Directions:

Preheat oven to 325°F. Bring 2 cups milk and rice to a boil in a medium-sized saucepan. Reduce heat, cover and simmer for 20 minutes. Remove from heat and stir in margarine. Combine eggs, milk, brown sugar, almond extract, cinnamon and nutmeg in a separate bowl. Gradually add rice mixture to egg mixture. Pour into a 10 x 6 x 2-inch baking dish. Bake for 30 minutes. Stir, sprinkle with pecans and bake an additional 20 minutes, or until knife inserted in the center comes out clean. Serve warm.

Yield: 6 servings
Preparation time: 1 hour

SWEET POTATO PIE

Ingredients:

1 9-inch pie crust, unbaked
2 sweet potatoes, baked
1/3 cup brown sugar
1 egg, beaten
1 tablespoon milk
1 tablespoon margarine
1 teaspoon vanilla
1/2 cup pecans, chopped
1/2 teaspoon cinnamon
1/4 teaspoon nutmeg
1/2 cup pecan halves

Directions:

Preheat oven to 325°F. Combine sweet potatoes, brown sugar, egg, milk, margarine, vanilla, chopped pecans, cinnamon and nutmeg in a medium-sized mixing bowl. Mix well. Pour into prepared pie crust. Sprinkle with pecan halves. Bake for 1 1/2 hours or until a knife inserted comes out clean. Cool.

Yield: 1 9-inch pie
Preparation time: 2 hours

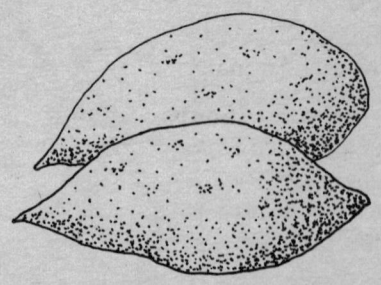

INDEX